Print information available on the last page

Rev. date: 06/05/2015

To order additional copies of this book, contact:
Xlibris
1-888-795-4274
www.Xlibris.com
Orders@Xlibris.com

My name is Teddy, but, I'm not a bear.
My name is Teddy, I have short hair.
My name is Teddy, I am a boy,
My name is Teddy, let's get a toy!

My name is Teddy, I love to run.
My name is Teddy, let's have some fun!
I said that I am not a bear,
I'm not a seal upon a chair.

But you can guess if you would like,
I'm not a monkey or a bike!
I'll give you hints to help you see
What kind of pet that I might be.

I have a tail, but I don't swing.
I have a voice, but I don't sing.
I can't climb trees or I would fall,
I can play with a tennis ball.

Since I can't climb, I'm not a cat,
I can not fly, so, I'm not a bird or bat
I have my meals out of a dish,
I like the water, but I'm not a fish.

I like the dirt, I like to dig,
But I am not a little pig!
I'm not a bug, I'm not a spider,
I do not like apple cider.

I'm not a lamb, I'm not a goat,
I'm not a pirate on a boat
I'm not a rabbit, not a bunny,
I think this game is very funny!

If you can't guess what I am now,
I'll tell you that I'm not a cow
I'm not a horse, I'm not a fly,
Take a guess, give it a try.

I like to play this little game,
cause all you know is my first name...
I don't live at the city zoo,
That is just a little clue.

I'm not a chicken or a duck.
So I don't quack, and I don't cluck.
I'm not a worm, I'm not a snake,
I live on land, not in a lake.

I'm not a toad and not a frog
I don't have bumps or sit on a log.
I'm not a hamster or a mouse,
But I do live in a person's house..

I can bark and I can howl,
And sometimes I can even growl.
My name is Teddy, as I said,
I have a very special bed.

Have you guessed my little game?
Now you know more than my name.
I am a dog I have to say,
I hope that you will stay and play

Printed in the United States
By Bookmasters